AF352183

Hold Me Steady, Lord

Hold Me Steady, Lord

AND OTHER PRAYERS FOR MOTHERS

Margaret B. Spiess

BAKER BOOK HOUSE
Grand Rapids, Michigan 49506

To my family
Erick, Anita, Gretchen, and **Marvin**
from whom I learned much
and who made the learning fun

I wish to thank
Jani Johnson, Kathy
Gouker, and especially
Genny Beasley, my secretary,
confidante, and friend.

How Should I Pray for My Children, Lord?

How should I pray for my children,
    Lord?
What I really want
is to keep them safe,
free from all danger, trouble, and pain,
wrapped in a warm cocoon,
or like a mother hen
keep them under my feathers.
Maybe I could give them a box labeled
What I've Learned About Life . . .
But they would emerge from the cocoon
peek out from the feathers
or ignore the box.

So here I am, Lord,
a mother beseeching for her children.
Be with them, Lord,
even when they think they don't need
    you.
You love them even more than I.
May they walk ever in the light of your
    presence.

"Serve the Lord with Gladness . . ."

"Serve the Lord with gladness . . ."?*
Most of the time I don't serve you at all,
   Lord . . .
My family
my friends
myself
but not you . . .
And almost never with gladness!
Why, Lord?
Why am I just skulking around the
   fringes of life,
not being particularly sad
but not radiantly happy, either . . .
just blah!

"Serve the Lord with gladness . . ."?
How?
Be a Pollyanna?
Be blind to the troubles I see?
Pat the victims on the head and say,
"It's God's will"?
Is it, Lord?
Or is our image out of focus?

*Psalm 100:2

Is the blessing we receive
related to our capacity to accept,
to be aware?
You came "that our joy might be full."†
Let me not limit that joy
by insensitivity.

†John 15:11

Tickleboxes
and Funny Bones

I could hug you, Lord, for creating
    laughter.
Thank you for giving me
a keen sense of the ridiculous
an easily toppled ticklebox
and a ticklish funny bone.

Thank you
for the joyous
contagious
healing power of laughter.

How Could I Be
So Blind?

I've hurt her feelings badly, Lord!
How could I be so thoughtless?
So blind?
Why couldn't I *see* she was eager for love,
for acceptance?
That she had something on her mind
that needed talking over?
She made a gesture of friendship
and I rebuffed it,
being so preoccupied with my own
    concerns . . .

She says it's OK,
but is it really, Lord?
She forgave me . . .
But she remembers
and I do, too;
she with chagrin
and I with embarrassment.

Where do we go now, Lord?
What can I do?
Perhaps our friendship is past reclaiming.

Please give her other friends who are
    thoughtful

and perceptive
and kind.
And keep me, Lord, from clumsily
    running roughshod
over the feelings of others.
Help me be kind rather than cruel;
grant me your concern for persons,
your empathy . . .
And forgive me, please.

I Must Get Rid
of These Grievances

I must get rid of these grievances, Lord—
have a funeral pyre and burn them all up!
I've hoarded them
as though they'd be of value someday
and instead they are making me ill.

Just now I saw a woman who wronged
    me years ago,
causing our family distress and loss.
My blood boiled and I trembled with
    rage.
(She didn't even see me!)
Why must I let her disturb me?
Why clutter my mind with this bitter
    memory?

Help me, Lord!
Let's gather these grievances together.
Cleanse my memories as I burn them
and guard me from gathering more.

True Self—Shrew Self

I expect to live to be an old, old lady,
   Lord,
but at the rate I'm going
no one will want me around!
There are those who could wish me
   departed now
or even last week
and I don't blame them.
Sometimes I can hardly stand myself!

When my Shrew Self gets the upper hand,
and I'm trapped on a treadmill of self-
   hate,
touch me with your love
and stop my senseless spinning.
Remind me
no matter how impossible I become,
I'm still worth reclaiming.
Speak from deep within
to comfort and calm me.
Only then
when I feel loved
can I love in return
and let my True Self shine through.

What's the Matter with Us, Lord?

Did you hear us just now, Lord?
Did you tune in on that exchange?
We sounded like two people
who hate each other thoroughly!
Impatient
gruff
demanding
petty
unyielding,
no softness of expression mitigating the
    harshness of tone.

What's the matter with us, Lord?
Deep down underneath it all
we love each other!
But sometimes the love is buried so deep
we almost ought to have a memorial
    service for it!
What makes us act like that?
Why don't I show courtesy to him
and he to me?
The same courtesy we accord friends
casual acquaintances
or even strangers?
Must we be so polite in public

that we have to blow off at home?

Maybe we need a reminder:
"Kindness spoken here!"
Let our love show in tone of voice
and consideration for each other.

Don't let us yell it to death!

And Then They Sang

We were all together after a lengthy
    absence
and there was much catching up to do.
Opposing viewpoints were challenged
    and defended —
and then they sang.

My heart filled with joy
and my eyes with tears.
For to me there is no sweeter sound on
    earth
than my children singing together.
Thank you for this precious gift.

Tired of Being a Mother

Sometimes I want to quit, Lord,
just go off and leave them to grow up
   alone!
I've done what I could.
(Not enough, surely,
often ill-advised and wrong,
but what seemed wise at the moment.)
How they turn out now is up to them
and you.
I'm tired of problems.
I resign!

Some mothers don't get so involved.
They say, "You handle your problems
   yourself.
I've done my part.
You're on your own."
But I wasn't smart enough to do that.
Are these children more self-reliant,
those families closer?

I don't understand, Lord.
Bear with me tonight
when I'm tired of being a mother!

The Question

I think I'll get a wig, Lord,
flaming hair to tumble about my
   shoulders,
add a beauty spot near one eye,
don a slinky blue dress,
and sport a slim, jeweled cigarette holder!
Do you think he'd notice?

I'm tired of being looked through
around
or over
as if I weren't there,
being regarded as comfortable
predictable
dependable!
(An old shoe feels great
but I never wanted to *be* one.)

I want to be admired
loved
share long, deep thoughts
and be appreciated for myself —
me!

What's that, Lord?
He sometimes feels the same?
Oh!

Lord,
help us!

Low Blow

That was a low blow, Lord,
a real low blow!
I'm still reeling under its impact.
What did I do to bring on this attack?
How did it happen?
You know my intentions were innocent,
that I "meant well" . . .

Somehow my words were grossly
  misinterpreted . . .
But that's all past now and the damage is
  done.
Forgive me for inciting anger in her, even
  unwittingly.

What must I do now to make amends?
You turned the other cheek, Lord,
but I'm unpracticed in cheek-turning
(and rather unwilling to learn!).
Still, this venom has an antidote
and the antidote is Love.

But how can I *love* her, Lord?
I don't even *like* her after this!
I want to fight back!
If it weren't for the others involved,
I'd at least write her off my list!

Knowing I'm hurt and angry
and reluctant to forgive,
will you still love me?
Will you help me *want* to want to love
    her again?
And because she may not give me a
    chance
to straighten things out,
I must be willing to remain in the wrong
    in her eyes.
Lord, if this proves so, I'll certainly need
to borrow your patience and
    understanding.
(I've none of my own in this.)

Help me, Lord, as I try to get
"sunny side up" again.

And help her, too.

A Driver's Prayer

I'm a potential killer, Lord,
because I drive a car!
My car, out of control,
can do horrendous things to the human
    body
even at fifteen miles an hour.

We intend to be careful, Lord.
The housewife hurrying to the store
before her company comes,
the husband dashing out for cigarettes,
the teen showing off for an admiring miss
all intended to be home for supper.
What innocent errands end in hospital
    beds
or in the morgue!

I want to be a safe driver, Lord,
to keep my car in good repair
be alert to changing traffic patterns
gauge other drivers' reactions
and respond quickly and wisely to
    emergencies.
When I'm unfit to drive with a blinding
    headache
drowsy from medication
overwrought

or overtired
let me surrender my keys.
But if I *must* drive
show me the best route
and guide my hands
and feet,
my thoughts
and my responses.
Steer me safely home.

Bless those who share the road with me
and most of all
drive with me, Lord.
Keep me from harming anyone
because I drive.

Culture Shock

I'm in culture shock, Lord!
The movie, rated PG,
showed bold intimate scenes between the
    man and the woman.
I don't want my children learning about
    sex
from the silver screen.

I taught them
and answered them
but how can I compete
with movie idols ten times life size
and in color?

And what of impressionable kids
who expect marriage to equal the
    exploits
of Sally Sexpot on the screen?

Keep my children straight, Lord.
Help them to know the deep abiding joy
as well as the palpitating heart.

Were You at Church Today?

Were you at church today, Lord?
Yes.
You were?
In my church?
I thought I was at a Kiwanis lecture.
And you blamed the minister?

Of course.

Did you go expectantly?
Did you arrive early enough
to settle down before the service?
Did you pray?

What I take to the service
determines what I receive?

Prepare me to receive the gift of yourself.
Make my heart an altar
and meet me there.

Marketing Day

Today is my marketing day, Lord,
but what can I buy?
The food never looked more tempting,
shiny scarlet apples,
golden lemons,
crisp green celery with manmade "dew"
    on it.
The very colors that make them attractive
may be dyes to poison the unwary.
I'm sick of worrying about DDT on
    produce
hormones in meat
mercury in fish
pesticides
additives
waxes.
Isn't *anything* safe any more?
(Fretting about cost, calories, and
    cholesterol is bad enough!)

What are we doing, Lord?
I thought we are our brother's keeper,
but quick profit seems the only motive
    here!
Save us from destroying ourselves
and each other.

Wake us in time
to save the health of our nation
and our world—
and help me as I shop for my family.

Volcano

I'm sitting on top of a volcano, Lord,
and it's set to erupt any minute!
There's a child who is depressed
one who's deeply hurt
and at the breaking point
and one whose feelings are tied so tight
    inside
I fear he'll explode.

I don't want anyone hurt, Lord.
I want to hold each of them close and
    murmur,
"There, there, it's going to be all right,"
and let them cry on my shoulder.
But they won't.

Would you enfold them, Lord?
So that they can feel your presence and
    your love?
Could you—even when they do not seek
    you?

Bumper Cars

Like bumper cars at an amusement park,
my thoughts jostle each other,
clamoring for attention.
The dark ones
      fear, doubt, frustration,
      anger, worry, resentment
vie with the light ones
      joy, faith, gratitude,
      love, hope, forgiveness
and those old standbys
      "It's just one thing after another,"
      "You can't win,"
      "Poor me."

But I have a choice,
and the decision I make affects
my family, my health, my pets,
and even my plants.
Help me select wisely what to focus on.

Generation Gap

I've taken too much for granted, Lord,
when I should have been thankful daily
that this child of mine is also my friend.

We've shared so much —
laughter
tears
secrets
high hopes
great dreams —
but the generation gap has reached us
and we've had a misunderstanding.

You who planned great things for her
when only you knew who she was,
guide her decisions.
Strengthen her steps
that she may walk with you
toward your goal for her life.
And show us how to be friends again;
I need her so!

Lonely Vigil

It's late,
really late, Lord,
and she's not home yet!
(What time *is* it?
I can't read the clock from here.)

I went to bed about midnight
and I've been asleep a long time
(or maybe just a little while, Lord?)
and she's still out!
Where is she?
Is she all right?
Did the car break down?
Is her date trustworthy?
Has there been an accident?
(Dear God, please, no!)
But where is she?

How can my husband sleep so soundly
when his daughter may be needing him?
Doesn't he know it's *late?*
(How late is it, anyhow?
I dare not disturb him to see . . .
but if I knew exactly, I'd know how much
    to worry!)

I hear a car slowing . . .
Is that them, Lord?

Oh, please . . .
But it passed on by.
Why doesn't she come home?
I know!
I'll try telepathy:
"Honey, come home!"
(It works for others —
why won't it ever work for me?)

I must have dozed . . .
I hear low voices on the walk.
She's home again!
Safe!
Thank you!
Thank you, Lord!
And thank you for keeping this
late lonely vigil with me.

Hound of Heaven

As the Hound of Heaven you pursue us
even when we flee your touch.
He's bolted, Lord,
but he needs you.
He thinks he's running distance
when he's really on a treadmill
circling round and round
going nowhere.

Break him out of the maze,
open his heart to hear your call
reach him
love him
heal him, Lord.

Betrayed

Lord, you didn't order your world
or the people in it
the way I think you should!

But help me realize you have the
   long view
and see forever.

When I'm disappointed,
let down,
betrayed by those I trusted,
let me remember
they're human
(thank God!)
and prone to error, too.

Since I often pay no attention at all
to divine prodding
and sometimes distress my friends,
help me to show loving-kindness
to those who disillusion me.

Take It Away, Lord!

Take it away, Lord!
Please take it away,
this mirror that reveals my soul;
I can't bear to look.

I thought my spirit was a bright and
    shining thing,
full-bodied and glowing with health,
not this ugly
shriveled
angry-red
clump!
But in the glass you hold before me
raw hatred and anger are revealed
and I shudder, knowing them mine.

I acknowledge the years of hiding
even from myself
my true feelings.
Resentments and bitterness?
Oh, I knew I harbored these occasionally
(Lord help me!)
but surely not this anger and hate!
Yet, here I am
stripped of my mask
no longer "sweet" and "patient"

while seething within.
What lies I've lived!

What now, Lord?
How do I make amends?

Bless first my unwitting victims;
grant them a special portion of
    your grace.
Then have mercy on me, merciful Father.
Replace the hate with love.
Let the moisture of my penitence
smooth out my wrinkled spirit;
breathe into it the cool breath of your
    forgiveness
and let it shine again
somewhere,
somehow!

Restore my soul, dear Father!

These Hands

These hands, Lord.
Thank you for these hands!
For these ten fingers which work together
or independently
and which can do many things.
No one has ever wanted to photograph
   them,
nor will they ever ask
(they are rough and blotched
and have too many burns).
But to me they're beautiful
because they work well.

Thank you that my fingers can write
   and type
crochet
plant a bulb
make cookies
sew a dress . . .

Bless my hands
that they may soothe the sick
comfort the despairing
pat a child
love my family.

Thank you for my hands.

At Ease

Why can't women relax with each
    other, Lord?
Why are we always making excuses?
Scarcely ever can one enter a house
without the hostess apologizing for its
    appearance,
especially if it shines like a new penny!
I don't see the fault till she mentions it
and then I can think of nothing else.

I'd relax and enjoy myself
if my hostess would allow it.

Sterile houses remind me of hospitals.
If real humans live there,
signs of their existence are expected.
I go to visit friends,
not to run a white-glove test!

Lord, teach women to be at ease with
    each other.

Thank You for Making Me a Woman

Thank you, Lord, that I wasn't born
  a man!
I love men, Lord.
I'm glad you made them.
But I'm glad I'm not one of them.
I don't have to be strong and brave.
I can cry and laugh and love
without being thought less womanly
  for it.

Bless men
for their strong shoulders to cry on
their bravery in the face of danger
their protection of women and children.

Bless my man, Lord.
I'm glad he chose me.
Help me to be more worthy of him,
more understanding and kinder
because I'm a woman
and a wife
and can express myself freely.

Ready for
the Glue Factory

My head aches, Lord,
and my feet hurt
and the points in between don't feel
    so well!
Some days I feel like I'm ready for the
    glue factory!

You didn't mean for me to feel this way.
You placed my soul in the perfect body.
If it's less than perfect now it's my doing:
overindulging in food or drink
    or emotion,
I have abused your temple.
I am heartily sorry.
Forgive me.

Place your soothing hands on my head,
my feet
and on the points in between
and show me how to accept your healing,
your love
and your forgiveness.
Show me how to be a good steward
of my body.

This Won't Do!

This won't do!
This really won't do, Lord!
My family works and plays hard
and at the end of the day they need a
   good meal
thoughtfully and lovingly prepared
served in pleasant surroundings.
Often they don't get it!

Sometimes I'm just too preoccupied
   to cook!
Knowing this, help me plan ahead, Lord,
so I won't offer my tired family
such a poor excuse of a meal as I served
   tonight.

Forgive me
and help me mend my ways.

Lucky

I'm one of the lucky ones, Lord.
Thank you! Thank you!
There was always someone to pray
    for me,
even before I was born.
And there have always been those
    who cared.

But it's not so with some of your
    children.
Millions have no one to pray for them,
no one to care whether they live or die,
no one at all!

Help us,
we who have been sustained by love,
upheld and nurtured by it,
to share your love
with the unloved
the unloving
and the unlovely.

Help Me Be Honest

"How well you played that piece!"
(When you should have been drying the
    dishes.)
"What a lovely dress you're wearing."
(I see you've no intention of vacuuming.)
"Yes, you may go to Margie's."
(But I wish you'd help me fold the clothes
    first.)

Why can't I say what I mean, Lord?
And why can't they see what needs to be
    done?
They always seem to have plausible
    reasons
for avoiding work.
(They must have a book,
*One Thousand Excuses for Every
    Occasion.*)
Why must *their* projects take priority?
I have hobbies, too.
Don't I deserve time for them?

If I'm honest, I'll admit I could plan
    better
and a little "meaningful dialogue" might
    clear this up.

Help me to be honest
with myself
with my family
with you.

Hold Me Steady, Lord

Lord, I need an anchor to hang on to,
the Rock of Ages to support me.
My world is shaken.
Future shock is here now
and I'm afraid.

What can I believe in?
Whom can I trust?
What can I do?
Where can I turn?

Hold me steady, Lord,
don't let me panic,
let me hold fast to that which is true.
"Whatsoever things are true . . .
are lovely . . .
think on these things."*

*Philippians 4:8

Fancy Sins

There's something perverse about me,
  Lord.
I'm almost jealous of those who make
  lurid headlines
with their fancy sins of the flesh!
Sinning on a grand scale sounds so
  exciting!
My sins seem tame by comparison
but they make a lot more people
more uncomfortable
than the publicized ones do!

Why is it, Lord, that "good" people are
  often sour
or surly
quick-tempered
unkind
uncharitable
or just plain blah?

We ought to radiate good nature
enthusiasm
happiness
and loving-kindness . . .
or at least be fun to be with!

I "oh" and "ah" at the headlines
because I'm blind to my own faults.
Let me be a good ad for my faith.
Show me how to be contagiously
     Christian.

Thank You for Caring for Me

I'm so glad I have you, Lord!
Often you're the only one who listens;
sometimes you're the only one who cares.
Thank you for caring for me.

I Want to Put Up a Sign!

I want to put up a sign!

EACH OCCUPANT OF THIS
HOUSEHOLD WILL BE EXPECTED
TO TALK WITH THE LADY
OF THE HOUSE
FOR FIVE MINUTES DAILY
AS A PERSON,
NOT AS A MOTHER-WIFE.
ANY SUBJECT ALLOWED.
HOWEVER,
REQUESTS AND COMPLAINTS ARE
NOT TO BE INCLUDED
IN THIS TIME.

Would that work?
Would they discover there's a mind under
  this thatch?
That we have more in common than a
  shared surname?

I like to feel important, too, Lord,
but I fade into the woodwork!
I spend half my time bolstering others'
  egos;
mine needs a little attention too!
I'd like a little stimulating conversation
now and then!

Show me how to cope with their
    unresponsiveness
to help them love me enough
to let me be my own unique self.

Crying Room

There should be a crying room at
    concerts
for people like me.
But the lights come on
and people start to leave
while I am still drying my eyes,
wanting only to retire to a dark corner
to let the beauty sink in.

Music moves me, Lord—
concerts of the masters
marching bands
joyous praise songs
even fluteophones.

Thank you for music
which lifts and stirs and gladdens
and thank you for the capacity to
    enjoy it.

I Prayed for Patience

I prayed for patience, Lord,
and I wish I hadn't!
Now I know we gain it
by having our patience stretched
almost to the breaking point
as mine is now.
I must keep quiet
but I almost choke
on words I want to say.

Do you almost gag
when we keep on in the same old sins?
Does your patience sometimes wear thin?

No?

Then I don't understand you at all, Lord,
not at all!

But there's Jesus!
He lost his cool a bit
there in the temple.
I'm glad I remembered
that Jesus was human and divine.
Help me as I seek to be like him
and thank you for letting me try!

Dialogue

Praise the Lord at all times!
When I'm unemployed
worried about money
anxious for the morrow?

Praise the Lord at all times!
When plans are thwarted
dreams destroyed
hopes crushed?

Praise the Lord at all times!
When disillusioned by a friend
disappointed
discouraged
blue?

Praise the Lord at all times!
When health is failing
hope flags
and death threatens?

Praise you, Lord?
Yes!
How can I?
Because I am.
Because I love you.
Because praise releases you to love me
  more.

Thoughts While Washing Dishes

Lord, it's been a long day
and I'm tired
and I don't want to do the dishes
(especially not alone!).
They've all gone off
on their own affairs
and left me with these messy plates
with food hardening on them,
pots to scrape and soak,
glasses with milk circles on them.
Ugh!
They seem to multiply as I look at them!

But wait, Lord,
we wouldn't have so many dishes
if we hadn't had a good supper!
We had variety
and abundance
and even some leftovers!

Thank you for the food that gave us
    energy
the appetite to enjoy it
the money that bought the food
the work that earned the money.

Thank you for water and soap
that make this dishwashing easier,
for the hands that can dispatch the job
in no time
if I just get at it!
Let me see these dirty dishes
as evidence of your abundance.
Even as I wash them I know that
when the next meal rolls around
I can pile dishes high again
and repeat the task!
I've never lacked for food
or been gnawingly hungry.
Thank you, Lord,
and give me a grateful heart
as I do the dishes.

I'm a Fraud, Lord

I'm a fraud, Lord,
an absolute fraud!
You and I know it
and I'm ashamed.
I'm like the little girl with a curl
right in the middle of her forehead.
When she was good, she was very, *very*
    good
(and I can put on quite an act, Lord!)
but when she was bad, she was *horrid*!
(That's me, too, Lord,
and often that's the side of me my family
    sees most.)

In public
with friends
attending church
serving on committees
I can be so "good" butter wouldn't melt
    in my mouth.
But there's my other self, just underneath,
angry
willful
impatient
self-centered
critical.

There's my pious side
and my private side
and they are poles apart!

For my family's sake
I wish it could be said of me,
"She was always best at home."
But I have a long way to go, Lord,
a long, long way!

Go with me, Lord,
and guide me
as I try to make what I am
and what I long to be
closer to your plan for me.

I've Done It Again, Lord

I've done it again, Lord!
How could I possibly take on all those
   jobs for *one* day?
Washing (remember my dryer's broken).
Chauffeuring the children.
Watching them perform.
Shopping for the week's groceries.
Finishing a dress for my daughter.
(Why do I promise and set times?
They're always so disappointed
if I don't come through.)
Preparing a special dinner.
Decorating a birthday cake.
The list is staggering.

I'm a fool, Lord.
I resent the demands on my time
(but I'm the one who offered!).
And I get so tired and cross
I almost ruin the event
I intend to make memorable.

Show me how to manage my time
or how to manage myself
to avoid undue rushing,
to enjoy the fun times I prepare for them.

And please, Lord, let the children remember
    remember
a calm, serene, loving mother . . .

Did you smile, Lord?
All right, I'll be honest.
Now and then
when I'm calm and loving,
could they notice and remember
and not think of me as always frantic,
please?

Have Lunch with Me

Will you have lunch with me today, Lord?
We're having avocado and sprouts
on pita bread
with a carrot/celery-juice chaser.
Not as tantalizing as a Reuben sandwich
and a Coke,
but it's as near to nature as possible.

I don't want to be a fanatic
but I don't want to feed my family
food that has been
mauled
injected
dyed.

Let me be willing to take a little extra
    time
to prepare fresh, healthful meals for my
    family.

Little Green Men

Some say there are little green men out
   there, Lord,
and maybe women, too?
Creatures with three eyes
and pointed ears?
Flitting about
flashing lights?
Signaling us, Lord?
Trying to be friends?
Wanting to show us what they've
   learned?
Wanting to help us?
(If we don't kill them first!)
It's exciting to think of life on Mars
or the other planets!
How wonderful it would be
if we could communicate lovingly
and learn to be One Universe
Under God!

Mother-in-law

When the minister pronounced them man
    and wife
he created a monster:
a mother-in-law.
Me!

I'm scared, Lord!
I like the man she married
and I plan to love him
when I know him better
but mothers-in-law are ogres
witches
interfering old biddies
according to tradition.
Might I be like that?

I want them to have a happy marriage
and a successful one
but I'm a mother-in-law
and likely to ruin the whole thing.
We'll have to work together on this,
    Lord.
Sometimes I'll be like a balky horse
whose tongue must be held with a bit
    and bridle.

Hold the reins tightly
and lead me away when necessary . . .

The state made me his mother-in-law;
will you make me his friend?

Moving Out

It's just an ordinary house
nothing fancy
nothing fine,
but the thought of leaving it
tears me apart.

It has seen many beginnings
and an ending or two
glad times
sad times
and times of deep contentment.

But since we must move,
send us a caring family
to keep these walls warm with laughter,
this roof a loving shelter
in times of pain.

Please send us, Lord,
someone to love our house.

I Nag My Children

I nag my children, Lord!
Constantly I harp at them:

"Why don't you do your homework?"
"Can't you ever clean your room?"
"Why can't you remember to do your
    chores?"
"Don't you ever think of anyone besides
    yourself?"
"You'll never amount to anything at this
    rate!"

When I listen to myself I get angrier
(is it any wonder they do, too?).
And when I really hear myself I
    become sad.

I sound like a harridan
without a shred of love in my heart!

I wouldn't be talking with you now,
    Lord,
if you nagged me like that.
If all you did was point out my
    inadequacies
(not to mention sins)
I'd feel crushed
unaccepted

unacceptable
a failure.

I'd feel no matter what I did
or how hard I tried
I'd never please you
so I'd quit trying
or maybe do things just to spite you!

Show me how to love my children as
    they are,
exactly as they are this minute.
They don't see things the way I do.
They may be worried;
they could be dreaming great dreams
or thinking long, long thoughts.

Let me see beyond petty annoyances,
    Lord,
guard me from stifling my children,
let me undergird them,
and may our home become a refuge,
a habitation of love.

Panic

Afraid!
Yes, Lord, I'm afraid again!
Yet!
Still!
I've tried Bible verses,
inspirational writings,
but where are the ones on sheer terror?
And why don't they speak to me?
Why do I have so many anxious days?
Help me.

"Perfect love casteth out fear."*

But my love is so imperfect, Lord.
I say I trust and then
when the crisis is over I say,
"Thanks, Lord, I'll take over now"
(as if I knew how!).
Or I prate about faith
while making myself ill with worry.

But wait!
Is it your love for me that casts out my
   fear?
Your love, spilling over,

*1 John 4:18

flowing into every nook and cranny of
    my being,
filling it so there's room for nothing else?

That's it, Lord!
Help me accept
without reservations
this marvelous gift.

Mustard Seed

Just as much as a grain of mustard seed.
That's all I need—
faith the size of a mustard seed
to remove this mountain
that obstructs my path.
I can see neither over it
nor around it.
To see the mustard seed
I almost need a magnifying glass,
but I've been magnifying the mountain!

Let me look beyond what seems to be
to what truly is.
Teach me to trust your Word
and rely on your promises.
Grant me mountain-moving faith,
    dear Lord.

Moving In

Everything is different here, Lord,
and strange
and we are far from the ones we love.
We sought your guidance in this move
but I wonder now if we listened well.
Guide us in this new place.

Lead us to the friends you have prepared
    for us
and let us prove once again that
"all things work together for good to
    them that love God."*

Hurters or Healers

We're all hurters or healers, Lord,
hurters
or healers.
Which am I?

I would be a healer, Lord!
Show me how.

*Romans 8:28

Martyr

If you ever run short of martyrs, Lord,
just call on me!
Oh, not the kind who die for a cause
but those who stand around muttering
complaining
and making everyone miserable.
I qualify . . . in every detail.
What makes me expect a gold medal
or a big hug for everything I do?

If I ask to be rid of this tendency
I would miss it
because I guess I almost enjoy being a
    doormat.
But I don't *want* to!
The me I really want to be
doesn't accept that trait.

Show me how to delegate responsibilities
and help me recognize my family's love
    for me
in small things,
even when almost covered by routine
or hurry
or absent-mindedness.

The Circus

The circus, Lord,
thank you for creating the circus!
Oh, I know you didn't design it
as part of your great achievement
in the beginning
but you put in someone's heart
all the zany
wonderful
fun ideas
that comprise the circus:
pungent animals
daring acrobats
capering clowns
and spritely circus music.

What fun to be a carefree child again,
spellbound by the ridiculous unreality of
   it all.

Bless the multitude of people
who live under the Big Top
and create the magic
of the greatest show on earth.
God bless the circus!

Just a Bundle of Nerves

How often have I heard
or said about another,
"She's just a bundle of nerves!"

Dear Lord,
often I'm rushed and nervous
but don't let me become
"just a bundle of nerves!"

Take care of my nerves, Lord,
and let me be a bundle of energy
a bundle of joy
a bundle of love
but not, please, ever
"just a bundle of nerves."

Gladness

How many times have I said,
"I'll be glad when . . ."?
I'll be glad when the baby sleeps through
            the night
            when the children can dress
            themselves
            when I'm done with carpools.

I'll be glad when I'm finished with PTA
            when everyone can type their
            own papers
            when I can wear size 12
            again.

But was I, Lord?
I forgot each time to be glad!

Teach me that the time to be glad is now
and the place to be glad is here.

In Advance

"Thanking you in advance," I wrote,
then sealed and posted the letter,
thinking happily of the arrival of the
    package,
confident that a complete stranger would
    honor my request.

But sometimes when I pray, Lord,
I have doubts.
I picture the worst,
as if I were petitioning a celestial Scrooge
reluctant to listen to my plea.
Now and then I worry when I pray.

Guide my thoughts and mental pictures
to fortify my prayers.
Let me anticipate a loving response
and help me to thank you in advance.

Wrong Number?

Today when I phoned my asthmatic
   friend
I got such a creaky reply
I urged her not to talk,
then had our prayer group remember her.

Later she called me,
hale, hearty, and vastly amused.
It had been a wrong number!

But was it, Lord?

Did that poor soul
need us?
Did you want special prayer
for that dear child of yours?
Bless that wrong number, Lord,
and let her feel your love.

My Finger's
Getting Numb!

Lord, my finger's getting numb!
I've held it in the hole in the dike
which protects our marriage
but it's getting cold and stiff.

Send help soon
before the levee cracks
and the floodwaters come,
washing away all our hopes and dreams
and our love for each other.

Let Go and Let God

Dear child, let go.
But my rope is so short and the fall
   so far.
Dear child, let go.
But I'm filled with fear and I'd
   rather wait.
Dear child, let go.
If there's no other way.

Dear Lord, I'm flying!
Why didn't you tell me I had wings?
You never asked, dear child.

My Rights

Lord, did I hear you correctly?
Did you say I have to give it up . . .
my "right" to be angry,
my "right" to be hurt?

But, Lord, everybody says I'm justified,
that they couldn't take it either.

Everybody?

No,
of course not you, Lord!

If I give up this "right"
I'll begin to see circumstances
and other people
with different eyes,
maybe even slightly the way you see
    them!

Wow!
Holding on to my "rights" was easier.
Help me as I give them up to you.

The Idiot Box

This box,
this idiot box!
Sometimes I hate it, Lord!
It brings into my living room
(frequently without warning)
words my family doesn't use
subjects I discuss only with my doctor
scenes which are offensive
broad double entendre . . .
even some of the ads should be restricted!

Every night
on almost every program
there's brutality
and violence.
Sex gets mistaken for love
and there aren't heroes any more,
only anti-heroes.

TV has great programs now and then
but meantime it's ever ready to hypnotize
indoctrinate
"inform."

I must not put my mind in drydock
because my body's weary.
Let me be discriminating in my viewing.

I've Wasted So Much Time!

Lord, I've wasted so much time!
I had a dream,
a goal I was reaching toward;
then
just as I could see progress
a huge obstacle loomed in my way.
It was like being in a dungeon
with only a glimmer of light
from the barred slit near the ceiling.
But there *was* light.

I've said, "I can't do it!
You see how impossible it is.
It was not my mission.
I'll have to give it up."

But maybe
though you didn't put this stumbling
    block in my way
you can use it to test how strong was my
    desire.
I need not look years ahead
but must walk toward my goal each day.
Forgive me for thinking it was too hard.

Thank you for the dream
and the means of making it come true.

Out of Focus

Lord, is that all she ever does—
pray?
Oh, I know we should
"pray without ceasing,"*
but really!
It bothers me.
You're always giving her messages
  for me.
Don't you
(please pardon my frankness)
ever tell her what to do
about herself?
And couldn't you be more direct
and give me my orders straight?

But unless she told me—
and she always does—
I wouldn't know she's one of your
  anointed
and not just an ordinary sinner like me.

Something's out of focus here,
Refocus us, Lord.

*Do you want refocusing, child,
or would you rather hang onto your peeve?*

*1 Thessalonians 5:17

A Multiple of Miracles

My body is a rainbow, Lord,
red, orange, yellow,
green, blue, indigo, and violet,
each cell radiant with the glory of
    the Lord.

Before I was born
my body formed and functioned and
    grew
according to divine plan.
Even now, its many intricate systems
    operate
without my conscious awareness
and healing is built in.

Thank you, Lord, for this
marvelous multiple of miracles
my own personal rainbow
my body.

Save the Children

I pray for the frightened children of
    the world:
neglected,
abused,
even starving;
for lonely latchkey children,
for those torn apart by battling parents,
for runaways.

To be a child today is to be a target
for all the sordid schemes man can
    devise.
What happened to childhood?
Save the children, Lord,
please save the children.

Water of Life

I've been using a medicine dropper, Lord,
taking the Water of Life drop by precious
   drop
as though by satisfying my need
I might deprive others.
But your gifts multiply with use
and are freely given to "whosoever
   will."*

I accept, Lord!
I plunge into the midst of the overflowing
   Fountain,
head thrown back and arms upraised.
Quench my thirst,
fill every cell of my parched being,
and make me whole.

*Revelation 22:17

Smog Alert

The air today is heavy and brown
and each breath sears the lungs.
Could I have caused some of that?

How often have I sullied the atmosphere
with my depression?
Inflamed my surroundings with my
    anger?
Weighed down the area with my fear?
Such attitudes are cumulative
and contagious.
Forgive me, Lord.

I like blue skies and clean air.
Help me do my part to provide them.

No Clones
in the Kingdom

Nothing in all creation
is a duplicate of its kind.
No leaf
no snowflake
no grain of sand
is exactly like another.

And since the beginning of time
there has never been anyone
quite like me,
nor will there ever be.
I am a unique
unrepeatable
irreplaceable
child of God.

Thank you, Lord,
for my own special corner
in your loving heart.

Friends

I feel warm
restored
comforted
equal to anything life might offer—
and all because of a visit from a friend.

When I needed someone to talk to
help with a problem
someone to cry with
someone to laugh with,
to share my distress
or my happiness,
you sent yourself
in the guise of a friend.

How blest I am.
How dear my friends.
Thank you, Lord, for each of them.

Dominion

In the beginning when you gave man
  dominion
over the earth, sea, air, and all therein,
all was fresh, pure, and beautiful.
We took these lavish gifts for granted
and tried to improve them
and now we have contaminated even
  space.

Forgive me for my part in this, Lord.
Point out what I can do to improve
  things.
Show me how to be a responsible tenant
  of this earth.

Attention!

Let me be attentive to those I love,
listen with hearing ears,
seeing eyes,
and a loving heart,
give myself wholly to the moment,
making sweet memories
as I go along.

Blessings

The stillness of a fern-carpeted forest,
the trusting curl of a baby's hand
around my finger,
the golden sweetness of apricots warm
    from the tree,
the crisp fresh scent of the air
after a thunderstorm,
my son's voice calling out,
"Hi, Mom, I'm home"—
thank you, Lord, for these comforting
    blessings.

A Thousand Deaths

Parents of kidnaped children
or runaways
must die a thousand deaths
watching, worrying, waiting, praying.
Strengthen them, O Lord,
and bring a blessing
out of all their sorrow.

Rules

My children sometimes think the
    rules I set
are from the age of the dinosaurs.
Help me discipline with kindness
rather than ultimatums,
assuring them of my love no matter what.

Devotion

He was the cleverest
and most interesting
man I knew.
So I married him
and waited for him to become
a storybook husband.

    He didn't.

Not for him were the dulcet tones,
hidden love notes,
unexpected gifts.

So, not seeing the forest for the trees,
I thought myself unloved.
How wrong I was!
His patience has sustained me,
his commitment has been my bulwark.
God bless this caring man,
my husband.

Hallelujah

Lord, I feel like giving you a big hug,
singing glad hosannas,
dancing in the street!
She made it.
She's going to be all right.
Hooray!
Hallelujah!
Praise the Lord!

Sleep

I lay awake last night and
today I'm complaining.
Since sleeping is what I do best,
I'm always annoyed to be wakeful.
But what if I spent the time praying,
sending arrows of love through the ether?
I'll try it next time around
and in the meantime,
I marvel at the miracle of sleep.

Entreaty

Dear Lord,
since you called him early
before the dance was over
before the race was won
only you know where he is.
Will you deliver this for me?

To Marvin
I never wrote a poem for you
who were a song and a poem to me.
Light, laughter, and love you brought us
and made each day a shining adventure.

My arms ache to hug you,
my ears to hear your voice.
Oh, my son, I miss you so.
How I love you.